science fair

Science Alive!
Magnets

CRABTREE
Publishing Company
www.crabtreebooks.com

How to use this book

Each chapter begins with experiments, followed by the explanation of the scientific concepts used in the experiments. Each experiment is graded according to its difficulty level. A level 4 or 5 means adult assistance is advised. Difficult words are in boldface and explained in the glossary on page 32.

Crabtree Publishing
www.crabtreebooks.com

PMB 16A, 350 Fifth Avenue,
Suite 3308, New York
New York 10118

612 Welland Avenue,
St. Catharines, Ontario,
Canada L2M 5V6

**Published in 2002
by Crabtree Publishing Company**

Published with Times Editions
Copyright © 2002 by Times Media Private Limited

Series originated and designed by
TIMES EDITIONS
An imprint of Times Media Private Limited
A member of the Times Publishing Group

Coordinating Editor: Ellen Rodger
Project Editors: P. A. Finlay, Carrie Gleason
Production Coordinator: Rosie Gowsell
Series Writers: Darlene Lauw, Lim Cheng Puay
Series Editors: Oh Hwee Yen, Scott Marsh
Series Designers: Loo Chuan Ming, Rosie Francis
Series Illustrator: Roy Chan Yoon Loy
Series Picture Researcher: Susan Jane Manuel

Cataloging-in-Publication Data
Lauw, Darlene.
  Magnets / Darlene Lauw & Lim Cheng Puay.
    p. cm. — (Science alive)
  Includes index.
  Summary: Introduces the concept of magnetism through various activities and
projects.
  ISBN 0-7787-0563-3 (RLB) — ISBN 0-7787-0609-5 (pbk.)
  1. Magnetism—Experiments—Juvenile literature.
  2. Magnets—Experiments—Juvenile literature. [1. Magnetism—Experiments.
  2. Magnets—Experiments. 3. Experiments.]
  I. Lim, Cheng Puay. II. Title.
  QC753.7 .L38 2002
  538—dc21

                                                    2001042425
                                                        LC

Picture Credits
Marc Crabtree: cover; Art Directors & Trip Photolibrary: 14 (middle), 18, 31 (middle); Bes Stock: 10 (bottom), 14 (bottom),
31 (bottom); Fraser Photos: 6; Hutchison Photo Library: 30; Liaison Agency: 19 (bottom); Science Photo Library: 1, 7, 10
(middle), 11 (top), 15 (bottom), 19 (top), 22, 26 (top); Tettoni Photography: 23, 27 (top);
Vision Photo Agency (S) Pte Ltd: 26 (bottom)

Printed and bound in Malaysia
1 2 3 4 5 6—0S—07 06 05 04 03 02

INTRODUCTION

What is a magnetic field? Why do magnets attract? Which is the strongest part of a magnet? Magnets are objects that can attract other objects. Today, magnets are used in almost every part of your home. Learn all about magnets by reading and doing the experiments in this book!

Contents

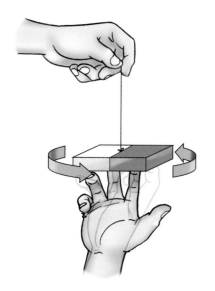

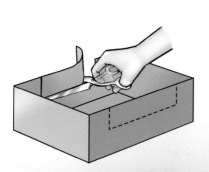

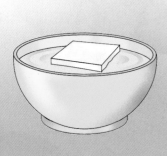

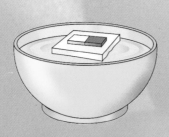

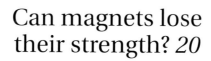

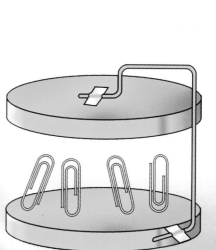

Magnetic forces

We can learn about magnets by looking at the objects they attract! Try to "float" some paper clips in this experiment.

Difficult – 5
 – 4
Moderate – 3
 – 2
Easy – 1

You will need:
- 4 inches (10 cm) of stiff wire
- Strong masking tape
- Two magnets
- Four to five paper clips

Dancing paper clips

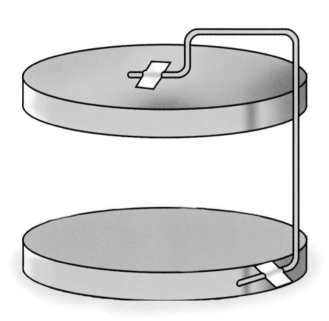

1 Bend the wire into the shape shown in the diagram and tape the two magnets to the wire. The opposite poles of the magnets should face each other. The magnets should be far enough apart so that they do not attract each other.

2 Place the paper clips on the bottom magnet. What happens? The paper clips stand up! The magnetic force of the upper magnet attracts the paper clips, but it is not strong enough to pull them off the bottom magnet. That is why the paper clips can stand.

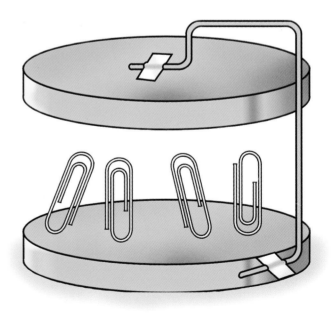

Here's a fun game you can play
using magnets!

Magnetic racetrack

You will need:
- Scissors
- A shoe box
- A sheet of paper
- Tape
- Plasticine
- Two rulers
- Two magnets
- Two paper clips

1 Use the scissors to cut out the sides of the shoe box as shown. Cut two strips of paper that are slightly longer than the box. The width of the strips should be about 2 inches (5 cm).

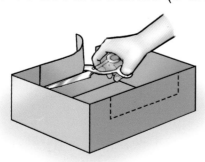

2 Tape the strips across the top of the box as shown on the right.

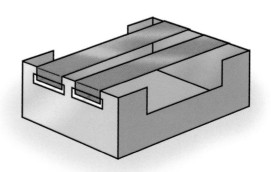

3 Put a piece of plasticine on the end of each ruler and press a magnet firmly into the plasticine.

4 Place one paper clip on each track. Use the force of the magnet to move the paper clip to the end of the track. Have a race with your friend. Can your paper clip make it to the end without falling off?

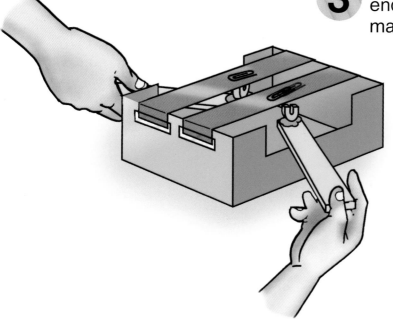

5

Magnetic forces

Every substance is made up of tiny particles called **atoms**. These atoms float around freely in an object, such as a paper clip. When a magnet comes into contact with a paper clip, the atoms of the paper clip become magnetized, which means that the atoms are pulled into organized rows inside the paper clip.

A magnet has a north and a south pole. Atoms also have a north and a south pole. Opposite poles **attract**, and like poles **repel**. In the *Dancing Paper Clips* experiment, the paper clips were magnetized. Their atoms were attracted to the opposite poles of the magnet, causing the paper clips to stand.

In the *Magnetic Racetrack* experiment, the paper clips were magnetized by the magnets beneath them. By moving the magnets, the attraction between the atoms of the paper clip and the magnets pulled the paper clips along.

Some traffic intersections rely on the interaction between metal vehicle bodies and electromagnetic fields to "sense" when vehicles are approaching.

How was magnetism discovered?

The term magnet comes from the word Magnesia. Magnesia was a region in ancient Greece where natural magnets were first found. Natural magnets are called **lodestones**. In 600 B.C., the Greeks found that rocks made of a mineral called iron ore could attract small pieces of iron. This kind of rock was called lodestone, or magnetite.

In the 1200s, a Frenchman, Petrus Peregrinus, became one of the first scientists to study magnetism. In 1269, he wrote an important book called *Epistola de Magnete*. His studies helped us to understand how magnets work.

QUIZTIME

What will happen if you place four pins on one end of a magnet?

Answer: The bottoms of the pins spread out. When the pins are magnetized by the magnet, a north pole and a south pole are created in each pin. Since opposite poles attract, all of the south poles at the top of the pins are connected to the north pole of the magnet. That leaves all of the north poles of the pins at the bottom. The bottoms of the pins spread apart because like poles repel.

Medical equipment called **bioresonance machines** (*below*) use magnets to help doctors diagnose patients' illnesses.

Did you know?
How do traffic lights "sense" when there are cars waiting to cross a traffic intersection? Intersections have coils of wire lying directly underneath the road. These coils of wire carry electrical currents and have a magnetic field surrounding them. When a large body of metal, such as a car, passes over the coil, it interacts with the magnetic field and changes the electrical current. This causes the traffic light to change!

MAGNETS AND PAIN RELIEF

You may have seen biomagnets for sale in shopping malls. Manufacturers claim that biomagnets help relieve pain. The magnetic force of these magnets improves blood circulation and causes blood vessels to expand. Some companies even make bioresonance machines that can be used to diagnose a patient's illness.

7

Opposites attract

Magnetic forces do not just attract things. Sometimes when two magnets are placed together, they move apart.

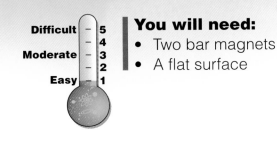

Difficult – 5
– 4
Moderate – 3
– 2
Easy – 1

You will need:
- Two bar magnets
- A flat surface

Magnetic forces

1 Place the two magnets on a table or any flat surface.

2 Slowly move the north pole of one magnet to the south pole of the other magnet as shown. What happens?

3 Now try joining the south pole of one magnet to the south pole of the other. What happens to the magnets?

Which part of a magnet is the most powerful? Does every part of a magnet possess the same magnetic strength? Do this experiment and find out!

You will need:
- A piece of string
- A bar magnet
- Paper clips

Magnet power!

1 Tie the piece of string around the middle of the magnet and allow it to hang freely.

2 Place paper clips on the magnet as shown on the left. The clips should be on both the north and south poles of the magnet.

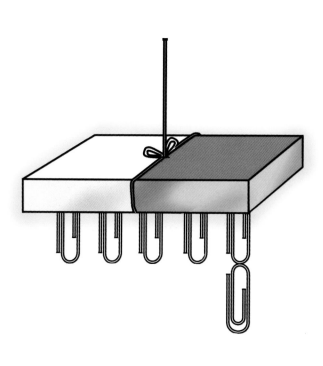

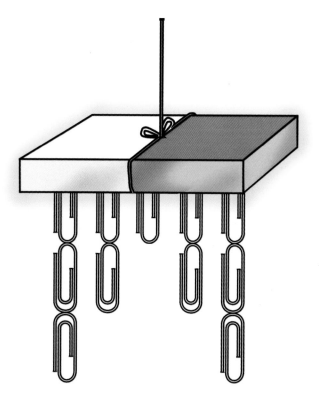

3 Slowly add paper clips until they start to fall off.

4 Which part of the magnet holds the most paper clips?

9

Opposites attract!

Magnets have a north and a south pole. Similar poles repel each other, while opposite poles attract each other. When we place the opposite poles (north and south) of two magnets together, they attract each other and join together. When the same poles (north and north or south and south) are placed together, the magnets repel each other and move apart.

The strongest part of a magnet

Every substance is made of atoms. Each atom has a continually moving cloud of spinning **electrons** around it. The spinning motion of each electron creates a magnetic force. This causes the magnetic fields in an atom to line up in the same direction and strengthen each other. As a result, the ends of the magnet have the strongest magnetic force (*left*). This was why more paper clips were attached to the ends of the magnet in the *Magnet Power* experiment. The middle of the magnet has very little, or no magnetic power.

Magnets come in different shapes. The long, straight ones used in the experiments are bar magnets. The one above is a horseshoe magnet. The north and south poles are located at the ends of the horseshoe.

Understanding magnetic forces

The ancient Greeks and Chinese knew about magnetic forces, but the reasons why magnets attracted other objects were not understood until 1925. Two American **physicists**, Samuel Abraham Goudsmit and George Eugene Uhlenbeck (*left*), showed that an electron spins. The spinning of this electrically charged particle causes it to behave like a small bar magnet. Their discovery helped us to understand how magnetism works.

Sue has two identical pieces of metal. One of them is a magnet. Without using any other object, can you help Sue identify the magnet?

Answer: Hold the two metals in the air to form the shape of a "T." The bottom piece of the "T" should be placed at the middle of the top piece. Let go of the bottom piece. If the top piece is a magnet, the bottom piece will fall off, since it was placed at the magnet's weakest point. If the bottom piece is a magnet, it will be attracted to the top piece as a magnet's strongest points are at its ends.

MAGNETS AND TELEVISION

Without magnets, we would not be able to watch television programs. The images on a television screen (*left*) are made up of millions of electrons hitting the screen's surface. The position of these electrons is determined by **electromagnets** in the picture tube.

Magnetic fields

H ave you wondered what magnetic fields look like? This exciting experiment will show you.

Magnetic field patterns

■ Ask an adult for help

You will need:
- An iron bolt or nail
- A metal file
- A piece of paper
- Two bar magnets
- Two pieces of white cardboard
- Clear glue

Difficult – 5
– 4
Moderate – 3
– 2
Easy – 1

1 Ask an adult to help you file the iron bolt, or nail, with the metal file. Collect the iron filings over the piece of paper. The file's surface may get hot, so be careful!

2 Place the bar magnets beside each other so that their opposite poles are facing. They should be far enough apart so they do not attract each other.

3 Place one piece of cardboard on top of the magnets. Slowly sprinkle the filings onto the cardboard. Tap the cardboard at the same time. What happens to the filings?

4 Arrange the magnets with the same poles facing each other. Repeat step three. What patterns do you see?

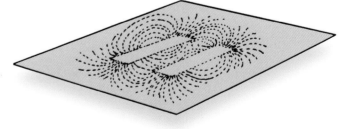

5 Spread a thin coat of clear glue over the other sheet of cardboard. Put the glued surface of the cardboard on top of the filings. When you lift the cardboard, the filings stick to it. You get instant magnetic art!

The pattern you see in the iron filings shows the magnetic field running from the north pole to the south pole of the magnet. This activity will show you the direction of magnetic forces.

The floating needle

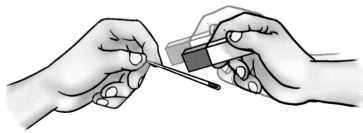

1 Stroke the needle lengthwise with the bar magnet. You should stroke the needle in one direction only.

2 Carefully insert the needle into the cork. Do not poke your fingers.

3 Tape the magnet to the outer edge of the glass as shown in the diagram.

4 Put the cork with the needle in the water. Place it near one end of the magnet and observe its path.

5 Repeat the experiment again. Does the needle always move along the same path? Why?

13

Magnetic fields

A **magnetic field** exists around a magnetic pole. A magnetic field is the area where the pull of the magnet can be felt. It starts from the north pole and moves to the south pole. The experiment with the iron filings showed the path of a magnetic field. The tiny bits of iron became magnetized when they were in the magnetic field, and lined themselves up along the field lines.

The floating needle

The floating needle in the water was influenced by the magnet at the edge of the cup. The needle followed the direction of the magnetic field—from north to south.

Compass needles (*above*) follow the path of the Earth's magnetic field.

Earth (*left*) has its own magnetic field. It is a giant magnet!

Measuring the magnetic field

The Earth is like a giant magnet. In 1750, John Michell, an English geologist, invented a device called a torsion balance to study small magnetic forces. Michell discovered that the strength of the magnetic fields between two magnetic poles grows weaker as the distance between them increases. His observations were later proven by the research of French physicist Charles Augustin de Coulomb.

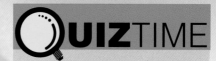
Did you know?

The human body generates its own magnetic field. The cells and tissues inside our bodies produce small electrical currents. Electrical currents create their own magnetic fields. Scientists using very sensitive instruments have detected the magnetic fields in our bodies.

METAL DETECTORS

Metal detectors (*left*) work similarly to traffic lights. The frame of a metal detector contains coils of current-carrying wire. Whenever metal passes close to these coils, the currents in the coils of wire will change, triggering an alarm. Metal detectors are often used to detect metals and weapons, such as **land mines**, hidden underground.

Making magnets and electromagnets

D o you know that you can use a magnet to make more magnets? This experiment will show you how.

Difficult – 5
– 4
Moderate – 3
– 2
Easy – 1

You will need:
- A pair of stainless steel scissors
- A bar magnet or horseshoe magnet
- Paper clips

Making a magnet

1 Take the scissors in one hand. Hold the magnet in your other hand. One of the magnet's poles should be facing the scissors.

2 Stroke the scissors with the magnet in one direction only.

3 After twenty strokes, use the scissors to pick up a paper clip. To increase the scissors' magnetic strength, stroke it again with the magnet.

You can use electricity to make magnets. Try this experiment and see for yourself.

Using electricity to make magnets

Difficult — 5
— 4
Moderate — 3
— 2
Easy — 1

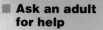 Ask an adult for help

You will need:
- Four to five paper clips
- An iron nail
- Insulated copper wire, 12 inches (30 cm) long
- A six-volt battery

WATCH OUT!

Do not leave the circuit on for too long! The copper coils will heat up, and you may burn yourself!

1 Place the paper clips near the iron nail. Are the clips attracted to the nail?

2 Coil the copper wire ten times around the iron nail as shown in the diagram.

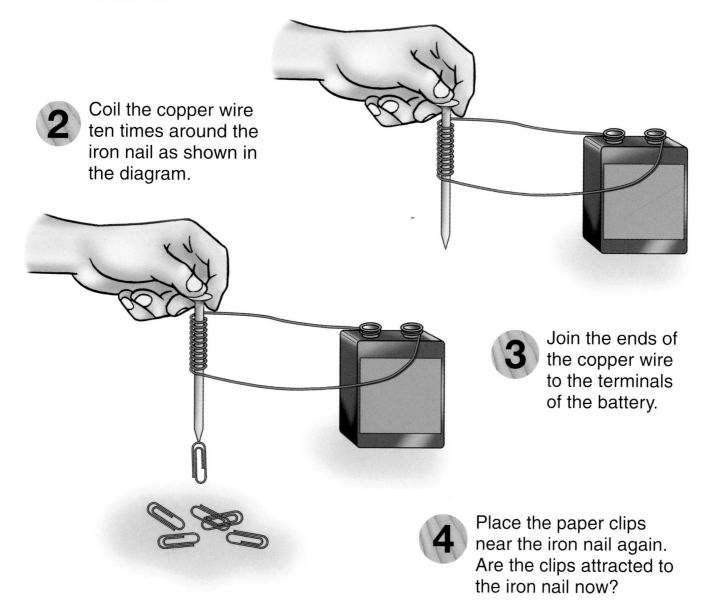

3 Join the ends of the copper wire to the terminals of the battery.

4 Place the paper clips near the iron nail again. Are the clips attracted to the iron nail now?

Making a magnet

Magnets have a magnetic force because the electrons in the magnet point in the same north–south direction. In the *Making a Magnet* experiment, the stainless steel scissors were not magnetic because the electrons in the scissors pointed in different directions. Stroking the scissors with the magnet caused the electrons to point in the same direction. This magnetized the scissors, which became a **temporary magnet** that would lose its magnetic properties after some time.

Electromagnets

A wire carrying a current has its own magnetic field. In the *Using Electricity to Make Magnets* experiment, the magnetic field made the electrons in the iron nail point in the same direction. This magnetized the iron nail. When the current was switched off, the iron nail lost its magnetic properties.

An electromagnet is attached to a crane (*below*). It is used to separate scrap metal for recycling.

Electricity and magnetism

In 1819, Danish professor Hans Christian Oersted (*left*) discovered that an electrical current flowing through a wire could move the needle of a compass. This discovery proved the connection between electricity and magnetism. Other scientists found ways to increase the magnetic strength produced by an electrical current. As a tribute to Oersted's pioneering work, the unit for measuring the strength of magnetic fields was named the Oersted.

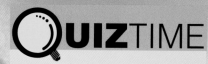
Did you know?

Electromagnets are used to lift heavy metal objects, such as cars, from one location to another. These magnets have many coils of wire wound around an iron core. When a current is switched on, the magnetic field generated by the wire is made even stronger by the iron core.

MAGLEV TRAINS

Magnets are used to make faster trains in Japan and Germany. Magnetic Levitation, or **maglev**, trains (*left*) use powerful electromagnets to lift the underside of the train up to six inches (fifteen centimeters) above special railway tracks known as **guideways**. Since the trains do not touch the guideways, there is less friction. This allows maglev trains to travel at speeds of up to 300 miles per hour (500 km per hour).

Can magnets lose their strength?

Magnets can keep their magnetic properties for a long time. There are ways to de-magnetize a magnet. Try this experiment to find out how.

■ Ask an adult for help

Difficult	5
	4
Moderate	3
	2
Easy	1

You will need:
- Some paper clips
- A bar magnet
- A piece of string
- A hammer

Removing magnetism

1 Suspend as many paper clips as you can on the magnet's poles. Record the number of paper clips each magnetic pole can support.

2 Ask an adult to hit the magnet at several places with the hammer. You can also drop the magnet on the floor.

3 Test the strength of your magnet again. Does it support more paper clips now?

20

We can also use heat to remove magnetism. Let's find out how!

Boiling magnets!

Ask an adult for help

Difficult — 5
— 4
Moderate — 3
— 2
Easy — 1

You will need:
- Some paper clips
- A bar magnet
- A piece of string
- A cup of boiling water
- A pair of tongs

1 Test the original strength of your magnet by using the paper clips as shown in the previous experiment.

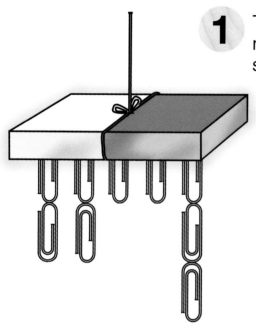

2 Ask an adult to help you boil some water and pour the boiling water into the cup. Drop the magnet into the cup of boiling water. Leave it inside for 20 minutes.

3 Ask an adult to help you take the magnet out of the boiling water using a pair of tongs. The magnet will be very hot, so do not touch it with your hands!

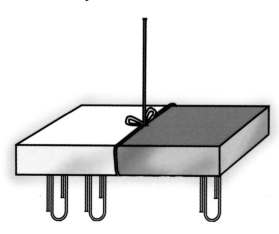

4 Test the strength of the heated magnet and compare it with its original magnetic strength. Is there a difference?

21

Removing magnetism

When a magnet is hit or heated, the positions of some electrons in the magnet change. Since some of the electrons in the magnet now point in different directions, the magnet loses its strength.

Speakers

Audio speakers use magnets to produce sound. The back of each speaker has coils of wire wrapped around a **permanent magnet**. This magnet is attached to a cone that vibrates according to the direction and strength of the electrical current passing through the wire. These vibrations produce the sounds you hear from your speaker.

Many devices in your home use magnets!

Heat versus magnetism

An English scientist, William Gilbert (1544–1603), discovered in 1600 that heating magnets caused them to lose their magnetic strength. This discovery was recorded in his book *Of Magnets, Magnetic Bodies, and the Great Magnet of the Earth*. The book described his research in magnetism and electrical attraction. Gilbert was the first person to use the term "magnetic pole." The gilbert, a unit used to measure magnetic force, was also named after him.

If you break a magnet into two, will you get two smaller magnets, or will the magnet be unusable?

Answer: You will get two smaller magnets! Even if you break a magnet, the alignment of electrons inside each piece is still the same. A new north pole and south pole will appear at the broken ends. This will give you two separate, but smaller, magnets.

Did you know?

The headphones *(right)* you use when you listen to music on a portable CD or tape player work the same way speakers do. The headphones have tiny magnets that help convert electrical signals into sound.

HANDLING MAGNETS

Magnets should be kept away from video or audio tapes. The tape's surface has a magnetic coating. When a recording is made, a tiny electromagnet in the recorder creates a magnetic pattern on the tape. If a magnet is brought close to the tape, the magnetic pattern changes. This means that the recording is erased, so you will not be able to enjoy the song or movie you recorded.

Magnets in our lives

Make your own doorbell to see how magnets are used in household appliances.

Difficult — 5
— 4
Moderate — 3
— 2
Easy — 1

◼ Ask an adult for help

You will need:
- Three pieces of copper wire, each 6 inches (15 cm) long
- Two thumbtacks
- Two erasers
- A paper clip
- A soft iron nail 4 inches (10 cm) long
- Tape
- A flat tabletop
- A six-volt battery
- Two metal strips from a paper fastener or duotang
- A screw 4 inches (9 cm) long
- The metal top of a bicycle bell, or a metal saucepan lid.

Ring the bell

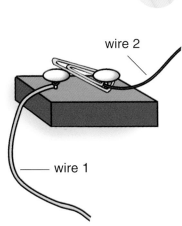

wire 2

wire 1

1 Wrap the ends of two copper wires (wires 1 and 2) around each thumbtack as shown on the left. Push the thumbtacks into one eraser. Attach the paper clip onto one of the thumbtacks. This is the switch for your doorbell. Place the switch on the table.

2 Coil wire 1 around the iron nail as shown in the diagram on the right, leaving at least 5 inches (13 cm) of wire 1 at its open end. Tape the iron nail to the tabletop.

NOTE

If the items are not available in your neighborhood's hardware store, ask your parents to suggest suitable substitutes.

3 Attach the free end of wire 2 to one of the battery terminals. Wrap one end of wire 3 around the other terminal.

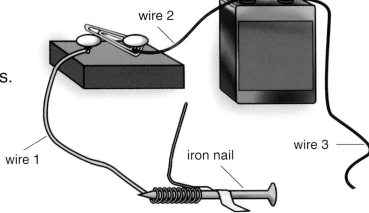

wire 2

wire 1

iron nail

wire 3

4 Bend one of the metal strips (A) as shown in the enlarged diagram below. Wrap the end of wire 1 around this metal strip and the other eraser. Tape the eraser to the table. The metal strip should not touch the tabletop.

5 Take the other metal strip (B) and coil one of its ends as shown below. Tape it to metal strip A.

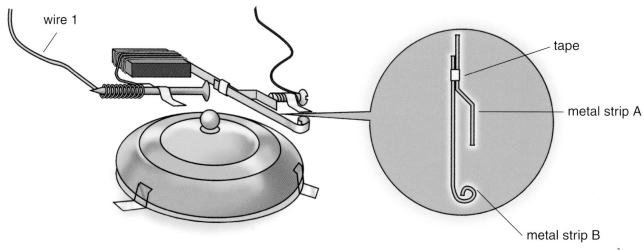

wire 1

tape

metal strip A

metal strip B

6 Coil the free end of wire 3 around the screw. Tape the screw to the tabletop next to metal strip A, but not close enough to touch it.

wire 2

wire 1

wire 1

wire 3

contact screw

7 Tape the metal bell cover to the tabletop. To switch your doorbell on, touch the paper clip to the thumbtack.

How electric bells work

When you switched your doorbell on in the *Ring the Bell* experiment, you created a closed circuit. This allowed an electrical current to flow through the wires. The wire wrapped around the iron nail turned it into an electromagnet. The metal strip was attracted by the electromagnet and moved toward it. The second metal strip moved with the first metal strip and hit the bell.

When the metal strip moved toward the electromagnet, it lost contact with the screw. There was a gap in the circuit, and electricity stopped flowing. The iron nail lost its magnetism and released the metal strip. The metal strip moved back to its starting position, where it made contact with the screw. This completed the circuit and allowed electricity to flow through the wires. The iron nail became magnetized and attracted the metal strip once again. This cycle was repeated until the switch was opened and electricity did not flow through the circuit any more.

General uses of magnets

Magnets are used for many things at home and in industry. Appliances in your home, such as tape recorders, refrigerators, and telephones (*below*) use magnets.

In industry, magnets are used to separate scrap iron and steel from garbage in trash sites so that the metal can be recycled. Power plants use large generators, which contain powerful electromagnets, to generate large amounts of electricity.

Did you know?

A magnetic strip can be found at the back of every credit card and Automated Teller Machine (ATM) card, or bank card. This is known as a **magstripe**. A magstripe has tiny magnetic particles inside a thin plastic strip. These magnetic particles send information to the credit card reader or ATM (*opposite*), such as the amount of money you have left in your bank account.

MIGRATING BIRDS

Birds such as terns fly to warmer places during winter. They can fly long distances without losing their way because they can sense the Earth's magnetic field. This is how they know exactly where they are going.

Transact

Making a compass

Sailors and explorers rely on compasses to move between different places. Now you can make a simple compass to start your own **expeditions**.

Difficult — 5
        — 4
Moderate — 3
        — 2
Easy — 1

You will need:
• A pail or bowl of water
• A piece of styrofoam
• A bar magnet

Finding your way around

1 Fill the pail, or bowl, with water until it is at least three-quarters full.

2 Put the piece of styrofoam on the water. Place the bar magnet on the styrofoam.

3 Observe which direction the magnet points in when it stops moving.

4 Repeat the experiment by turning the piece of styrofoam around. Does the magnet always point in the same direction when it stops? Why?

If you do not have a pail, or bowl, of water or a piece of styrofoam, a piece of string will do just as well.

Difficult — 5
— 4
Moderate — 3
— 2
Easy — 1

You will need:
• A piece of string
• A bar magnet

Aerial compass

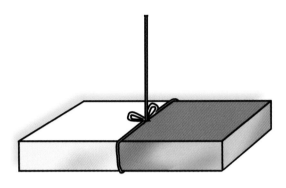

1 Tie the piece of string to the middle of the bar magnet as shown.

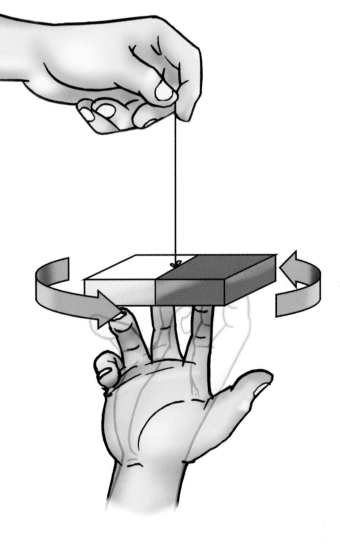

2 Hold the string and allow the magnet to hang freely in the air. Note which direction the magnet is pointing in when it stops moving.

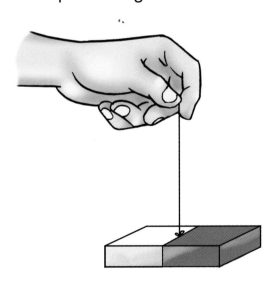

3 Spin the magnet around again. Does the magnet point in the same direction when it stops spinning?

Earth: the largest magnet of all

The magnet floating on the water or suspended by the string was influenced by the magnetic field of a giant magnet—Earth. The Earth is actually a large magnet with north and south magnetic poles. This explains why a magnet follows a north–south direction. Magnets are used in compasses to tell sailors and pilots which direction they are headed.

Some scientists believe that the Earth's magnetic field is created by molten iron that is deep under the ground. The movement of the iron creates electricity. Electrical charges lead to the creation of a magnetic field.

Compasses and other computer systems help pilots (*below*) find their way around in the sky.

History of compasses

During the **Middle Ages**, simple compasses were made by attaching pieces of lodestone to wooden splints floating on bowls of water. Since lodestones are natural magnets, they point in a north–south direction. They helped sailors find their way in the world's oceans. These simple devices were the ancestors of modern aircraft and ship compasses.

Did you know?

When a volcano erupts (*right*), fiery rivers of molten lava pour out. Molten lava contains iron. As the hot lava cools into rock, the rock is magnetized in the direction of the Earth's magnetic field.

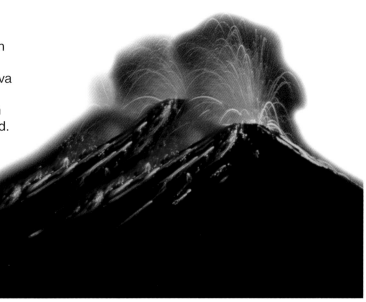

LIFE-SAVING MAGNETISM

The Earth's magnetic field is also a protective layer. It helps deflect harmful particles from the sun. These particles contain radiation and will harm us if we are exposed to them for a long time.

31

Glossary

atom (page 6): The smallest particle found in any object.

attract (page 6): To pull toward.

bioresonance machine (page 7): A machine that detects a person's electromagnetic field. These machines are used in the treatment of illnesses.

electromagnet (page 11): A device with a core made from magnetic material surrounded by a coil of wire. An electrical current is passed through the coil to magnetize the core.

electrons (page 10): Particles that are negatively charged.

expedition (page 28): A journey taken for a specific purpose, such as finding buried treasure or a sunken ship.

guideways (page 19): Special tracks that magnetic levitation (maglev) trains use to move on. Maglev trains cannot run on normal railroad tracks.

land mine (page 15): A deadly weapon that explodes when a person steps on it.

lodestone (page 7): A natural magnet that is a stone made from magnetite.

maglev (page 19): Magnetic levitation trains that use electromagnetic energy to move above special tracks.

magnetic field (page 14): The space near a body or magnetic pole where magnetic forces can be detected.

magstripe (page 27): The thin strip of magnetic material found on credit and ATM cards.

Middle Ages (page 31): The period in European history between 400 A.D. and the early 1400s.

permanent magnet (page 22): A magnet that keeps its magnetic properties.

phycisist (page 11): A scientist who specializes in the study of physics.

repel (page 6): To push back.

temporary magnet (page 18): A magnet that loses all or most of its magnetic properties after some time.

Index